Lent and Easter Prayer Guide 2025

A Journey of Renewal and Spiritual Growth

Jesse Lawrence

Copyright © 2025 Jesse Lawrence
It is not legal to reproduce, duplicate, or transmit any part of this document in either electronic means or in printed format. Recording of this publication is strictly prohibited.

TABLE OF CONTENT

Introduction	3
Ash Wednesday & the First Week of Lent	6
Ash Wednesday: Embracing Mortality, Embracing Hope	6
Day 1: Finding God in the Silence	8
Day 2: The Healing Power of Forgiveness	10
Day 3: Embracing Simplicity	11
Day 4: Listening to the Word	12
Day 5: Extending a Hand of Mercy	13
Day 6: Surrendering to God's Will	14
Day 7: Renewing Our Commitment	15
The Second Week of Lent	16
Day 8: Resisting Temptation, Embracing Virtue	16
Day 9: Cultivating Gratitude	18
Day 10: Finding Joy in the Present Moment	19
Day 11: Trusting in God's Providence	20
Day 12: Letting Go of Control	21
Day 13: The Healing Power of Forgiveness	22
Day 14: Discovering God's Love in Creation	23
The Third Week of Lent	24
Day 15: Walking with Jesus in the Desert	24
Day 16: The Power of Christian Community	26
Day 17: Praying for the Needs of the World	27
Day 18: Cultivating Compassion	28
Day 19: Seeking Justice and Peace	29
Day 20: Finding Strength in Weakness	30
Day 21: Preparing for Holy Week	31

Holy Week	32
Palm Sunday: Joy, Humility, and the Cost of Discipleship	32
Holy Monday & Tuesday: Betrayal and the Sacrament of Love	34
Holy Wednesday: Silence and Reflection	36
Maundy Thursday: Service and Communion	37
Good Friday: Contemplating the Cross	38
Holy Saturday: Hope in Darkness	39
Easter Sunday	40
Easter Sunday: Celebrating the Resurrection	40
Easter Monday: Living the Resurrected Life	41

Introduction

Rain lashed against the windowpane, mirroring the storm brewing within my soul. It was the eve of Ash Wednesday, and a profound sense of unease had settled over me. I felt adrift, my faith a distant memory, buried beneath the weight of daily anxieties and the relentless demands of life.

I longed for a deeper connection with God, a way to break free from the distractions that had consumed me. Lent, I knew, offered a sacred space for such a journey – a time to turn inward, to shed the layers of complacency, and to rediscover the transformative power of faith.

But where to begin? The weight of tradition, the expectations of others, and the sheer volume of spiritual resources felt overwhelming. I yearned for a guide, a companion to walk with me through this sacred season, a beacon of light in the darkness.

And so, I embarked on a journey of my own, seeking a way to make Lent truly meaningful. I delved into ancient texts, explored diverse spiritual traditions, and sought wisdom from those who had walked this path before. I discovered that Lent, at its heart, is a deeply personal journey, a time for introspection and renewal. It is a season to cultivate a deeper relationship with God, to embrace simplicity, and to extend compassion to others.

This guide is born from that journey, a testament to the transformative power of Lent. It is an invitation to join me on a path of spiritual exploration, a companion to guide you through the forty days of reflection and renewal.

We will begin with Ash Wednesday, a poignant reminder of our mortality and a call to repentance. We will journey through the weeks of Lent, exploring themes of temptation, forgiveness, and the importance of community. We will look into the profound mysteries of Holy Week, culminating in the triumphant celebration of Easter Sunday.

Each day, you will find a reflection on a specific theme or biblical passage, designed to inspire contemplation and deepen your understanding of the Lenten journey. You will also encounter a selection of prayers, meditations, and spiritual practices to nourish your soul and guide you on your path.

This guide is not meant to be a rigid set of rules or a prescriptive program. Rather, it is a flexible framework, a starting point for your own unique Lenten experience. Feel free to adapt it to your own needs and circumstances, to explore the themes that resonate most deeply with you, and to create your own sacred space for prayer and reflection.

Let us embark on this journey together, with open hearts and minds. Let us shed the weight of our burdens and embrace the grace of God. Let us use this sacred season to rediscover the depths of our faith and to emerge from Lent renewed, refreshed, and ready to embrace the joys of the resurrection.

Ash Wednesday & the First Week of Lent

Ash Wednesday: Embracing Mortality, Embracing Hope

Today, as we receive the sign of the cross upon our foreheads, we are reminded of our mortality, "Remember that you are dust, and to dust you shall return." (Genesis 3:19). This poignant reminder of our fleeting existence can be a source of profound sorrow, but also a powerful invitation to deeper meaning.

Ash Wednesday calls us to examine our lives, to acknowledge our shortcomings, and to turn back to God. It is a time for repentance, for turning away from sin and embracing a life of love and service. But repentance is not simply about feeling sorry for our mistakes. It is about a deep and sincere desire to change, to align our lives more closely with God's will.

As you receive the ashes today, take a moment to reflect on your own mortality. Consider the fleeting nature of time and the preciousness of each moment. Allow this awareness to awaken a sense of urgency within you.

Use this Lenten season to cultivate a deeper relationship with God, to embrace simplicity, and to extend love and compassion to those around you.

Prayer for Ash Wednesday:

- *Loving God, as I receive the ashes today, I humbly acknowledge my mortality. Forgive me for my sins and shortcomings. Help me to turn away from the things that distract me from you and to embrace a life of love and service. Amen.*

Day 1: Finding God in the Silence

In the hustle and bustle of our daily lives, it can be difficult to find time for quiet reflection. Yet, it is in the stillness that we often encounter God most deeply. Today, let us carve out some time for solitude. Find a quiet place where you can be alone with your thoughts and connect with God.

- **Creating a Quiet Space:**
    - Choose a place where you will not be disturbed. It could be a corner of your bedroom, a quiet spot in nature, or a designated prayer corner in your home.
    - Clear the space of distractions. Turn off your phone, put away any unnecessary items, and light a candle if you wish.
    - Create a comfortable atmosphere. Sit or kneel in a position that allows you to be still and attentive.
- **Practices for Solitude:**
    - **Lectio Divina:** This ancient practice involves slowly reading a passage of Scripture, pondering its meaning, and

allowing God's word to speak to your heart.
- **Contemplative Prayer:** This simple yet profound practice involves sitting quietly and focusing your attention on God's presence. You may find it helpful to repeat a short prayer or mantra, such as "Come, Lord Jesus."

- **Prayer for Solitude:**

  - *Lord, grant me the grace to find stillness within myself. Help me to quiet my mind and open my heart to your presence. May I encounter you in the silence, and may my soul be refreshed by your love. Amen.*

Day 2: The Healing Power of Forgiveness

Forgiveness is not always easy. It may require us to confront painful memories, to let go of resentment, and to extend grace to those who have hurt us. Yet, forgiveness is essential for our own healing and for our relationship with God.

Forgiveness is not just about forgiving others. It is also about forgiving ourselves. We all make mistakes, and it is important to learn from them and move on. Extend compassion to yourself and acknowledge your own need for grace.

- **Practicing Acts of Reconciliation:**
    - If you have wronged someone, reach out and apologize sincerely.
    - If you have been hurt by someone, try to understand their perspective and offer forgiveness.
    - Practice acts of kindness and compassion towards others.
- **Prayer for Forgiveness:**
    - *Lord, forgive me for my sins and shortcomings. Help me to forgive those who have hurt me, and to offer myself the grace and compassion I need to heal. Amen.*

Day 3: Embracing Simplicity

In our consumer-driven world, it can be easy to get caught up in the pursuit of material possessions and fleeting pleasures. Lent is a time to embrace simplicity, to let go of distractions, and to focus on what truly matters.

- **Simplifying Daily Life:**
    - Declutter your home and donate unwanted items.
    - Limit your screen time and spend more time in nature.
    - Practice mindful eating and drinking.
    - Simplify your daily routine and focus on what is truly essential.
- **Prayer for Simplicity:**
    - *Lord, help me to detach from the things that distract me from you. Grant me the grace to live simply and to focus on what truly matters. Amen.*

Day 4: Listening to the Word

The Bible is the Word of God, a source of wisdom, guidance, and inspiration. During Lent, let us make a conscious effort to spend more time with Scripture.

- **Engaging with Scripture:**

    - **Daily Readings:** Set aside some time each day to read a passage from the Bible.
    - **Journaling:** Reflect on your readings and write down your thoughts and insights.
    - **Bible Study:** Join a Bible study group or attend a church service where the Bible is taught.
- **Prayer for Understanding:**

    - *Lord, open my heart and mind to your Word. Help me to understand your teachings and to apply them to my life. Amen.*

Day 5: Extending a Hand of Mercy

Lent is a time to put our faith into action. We are called to be instruments of God's love and compassion in the world.

- **Practicing Acts of Mercy:**

    - Volunteer at a local soup kitchen or homeless shelter.
    - Visit the sick or elderly.
    - Donate to a charitable organization.
    - Offer a helping hand to a neighbor or friend in need.
- **Prayer for Opportunities to Serve:**

    - *Lord, open my eyes to the needs of those around me. Grant me the opportunity to serve you by serving others. Amen.*

Day 6: Surrendering to God's Will

Surrendering our will to God is not always easy. It requires us to trust in God's plan, even when we do not understand it.

- **Trusting in God's Guidance:**
    - Spend time in prayer, asking God for guidance and direction.
    - Be open to unexpected opportunities and challenges.
    - Remember that God is always with you, even in the midst of uncertainty.
- **Prayer for Surrender:**
    - *Lord, I surrender my will to yours. Help me to trust in your plan for my life, even when I cannot see the path ahead. Amen.*

Day 7: Renewing Our Commitment

Lent is a time for renewal and recommitment to our faith. Let us use this season to rededicate ourselves to God and to the call to discipleship.

- **Renewing Baptismal Vows:**

    - Reflect on your baptismal promises and recommit yourself to living a life that reflects your faith.
- **Recommitting to Discipleship:**

    - Seek ways to grow in your faith through prayer, study, and service.
    - Share your faith with others and be a witness to the love of God.
- **Prayer for Renewal:**

    - *Lord, renew my faith and strengthen my commitment to you. Help me to live a life that reflects your love and grace. Amen.*

This is just a starting point for your Lenten journey. May God bless you as you seek to deepen your relationship with Him during this sacred season

The Second Week of Lent

Day 8: Resisting Temptation, Embracing Virtue

Temptation is a constant in our lives. Whether it's the allure of worldly pleasures, the pressure to conform, or the pull of negative emotions, we all face challenges that test our faith and our commitment to God.

This week, let us reflect on the nature of temptation and explore strategies for resisting it.

- **Recognizing Temptation:**
    - Become aware of the temptations you face most often.
    - Identify the triggers that lead to these temptations.
    - Acknowledge the underlying desires that fuel these temptations.
- **Cultivating Virtue:**
    - Focus on cultivating virtues such as humility, patience, and self-control.
    - Surround yourself with supportive friends and mentors.

- Engage in activities that nourish your soul and strengthen your relationship with God.
- **Prayer for Strength:**
  - *Lord, help me to resist temptation and to walk in your ways. Grant me the strength to overcome sin and to live a life that reflects your love. Amen.*

Day 9: Cultivating Gratitude

In the midst of our busy lives, it's easy to lose sight of the many blessings we have received. This week, let us cultivate a spirit of gratitude.

- **Practicing Gratitude:**
    - Keep a gratitude journal and write down things you are thankful for each day.
    - Express your thanks to others for their kindness and support.
    - Take time to appreciate the beauty of nature and the simple joys of life.
- **Prayer of Thanksgiving:**
    - Lord, I thank you for all your blessings. Thank you for your love, your mercy, and your grace. Help me to cultivate a spirit of gratitude and to live a life of thanksgiving. Amen.

Day 10: Finding Joy in the Present Moment

In our pursuit of happiness, we often find ourselves chasing after fleeting pleasures or dwelling on past regrets. This week, let us practice finding joy in the present moment.

- **Mindfulness and Presence:**

    - Practice mindfulness meditation, focusing on your breath and the sensations of your body.
    - Engage fully in the activities you are doing, whether it's eating a meal, listening to music, or spending time with loved ones.
    - Appreciate the beauty of the present moment and savor each experience.
- **Prayer for Joy and Peace:**

    - *Lord, help me to find joy in the present moment. Grant me the peace that surpasses all understanding and the ability to savor each day as a gift. Amen.*

Day 11: Trusting in God's Providence

Life is full of uncertainties and challenges. It can be difficult to let go of control and trust in God's plan. This week, let us practice surrendering our anxieties and trusting in God's loving care.

- **Surrendering to God's Will:**
    - Spend time in prayer, acknowledging your dependence on God.
    - Remember that God is always with you, even in the midst of difficulty.
    - Trust that God will work all things together for good.
- **Prayer for Trust and Peace of Mind:**
    - *Lord, I surrender my anxieties and worries to you. Help me to trust in your loving care and to find peace in your presence. Amen.*

Day 12: Letting Go of Control

Our desire for control can often lead to stress and anxiety. This week, let us practice letting go of control and embracing uncertainty.

- **Embracing Uncertainty:**

    - Acknowledge that you cannot control everything in your life.
    - Learn to accept the unexpected and embrace change.
    - Trust that God is in control and that all things will work out according to His plan.
- **Prayer for Surrender and Acceptance:**

    - *Lord, help me to let go of my need for control. Grant me the grace to accept uncertainty and to trust in your loving guidance. Amen.*

Day 13: The Healing Power of Forgiveness

Forgiveness is a gift we give ourselves as much as it is a gift we give to others. It is a powerful act of healing that can free us from the burdens of resentment and anger.

- **Forgiving Yourself and Others:**
    - Acknowledge your own shortcomings and forgive yourself for your mistakes.
    - Extend forgiveness to those who have hurt you, even if they do not deserve it.
    - Practice acts of kindness and compassion towards others.
- **Prayer for Forgiveness and Healing:**
    - *Lord, help me to forgive myself and others. Heal the wounds of the past and grant me the freedom that comes with forgiveness. Amen.*

Day 14: Discovering God's Love in Creation

Nature is a manifestation of God's creative power and a source of wonder and awe. This week, let us spend time in nature and appreciate the beauty of God's creation.

- **Connecting with Nature:**
    - Take a walk in the park, go for a hike, or simply spend time in your garden.
    - Observe the beauty of the natural world – the trees, the flowers, the animals.
    - Give thanks for the wonders of creation and the love of God that is revealed in all things.
- **Prayer for Gratitude for Creation:**
    - *Lord, I thank you for the beauty and wonder of your creation. Help me to appreciate the natural world and to see your love reflected in all things. Amen.*

The Third Week of Lent

Day 15: Walking with Jesus in the Desert

Just as Jesus faced temptation and hardship in the desert, we too may encounter challenges and trials during our Lenten journey. This week, let us reflect on the importance of spiritual discipline and facing challenges with faith.

- **Embracing Spiritual Discipline:**
    - Set aside dedicated time for prayer and reflection each day.
    - Fast or abstain from certain activities as a way of deepening your spiritual practice.
    - Engage in acts of self-denial to cultivate humility and focus on God.
- **Facing Challenges with Faith:**
    - Remember that God is always with you, even in the midst of difficulty.
    - Turn to Scripture and prayer for guidance and strength.

- Seek support from your faith community.
- **Prayer for Strength and Perseverance:**

  - *Lord, grant me the strength and perseverance to face the challenges of this Lenten journey. Help me to walk with you through the desert and to emerge stronger in my faith. Amen.*

Day 16: The Power of Christian Community

We are not meant to walk this journey alone. The Christian community provides us with support, encouragement, and a shared sense of purpose. This week, let us reflect on the importance of connecting with other believers.

- **Building Christian Community:**
    - Attend church services and participate in church activities.
    - Join a small group or Bible study.
    - Reach out to other Christians for support and encouragement.
    - Serve others alongside your fellow believers.
- **Prayer for Christian Community:**
    - *Lord, help me to connect with other believers and to build a strong and supportive Christian community. May we love one another as you have loved us. Amen.*

Day 17: Praying for the Needs of the World

As followers of Christ, we are called to be concerned with the well-being of all people. This week, let us spend time in prayer for the needs of the world.

- **Praying for Global Solidarity:**

    - Pray for an end to poverty, hunger, and disease.
    - Pray for justice and peace in all nations.
    - Pray for the protection of the environment and the well-being of all creation.
- **Prayer for the Needs of the World:**

    - *Lord, have mercy on the world. Heal the divisions that separate us and grant us the courage to work for justice and peace. Amen.*

Day 18: Cultivating Compassion

Compassion is the heart of the Christian faith. It is the ability to understand and share the feelings of others, and to act with kindness and mercy. This week, let us cultivate a spirit of compassion in our own lives.

- **Showing Kindness to Others:**
    - Offer a helping hand to someone in need.
    - Listen with empathy to the struggles of others.
    - Practice acts of kindness and compassion in our daily lives.
- **Prayer for Compassion and Love:**
    - *Lord, fill my heart with compassion and love. Help me to see the needs of others and to respond with kindness and mercy. Amen.*

Day 19: Seeking Justice and Peace

As followers of Christ, we are called to work for justice and peace in the world. This week, let us reflect on our role in advocating for a more just and equitable society.

- **Advocating for Social Justice:**
    - Support organizations that work for social justice.
    - Speak out against injustice and inequality.
    - Use your voice and your resources to make a difference in the world.
- **Prayer for Justice and Peace:**
    - *Lord, grant us the courage to work for justice and peace in the world. Help us to build a more just and equitable society where all people can live in dignity and freedom. Amen.*

Day 20: Finding Strength in Weakness

We all experience times of weakness and vulnerability. This week, let us reflect on the importance of acknowledging our limitations and relying on God's grace.

- **Relying on God's Grace:**

    - Acknowledge your own weaknesses and limitations.
    - Turn to God for strength and support.
    - Remember that God's grace is sufficient for you.
- **Prayer for Strength and Grace:**

    - *Lord, I acknowledge my weakness and my need for your grace. Help me to rely on you in all things and to find strength in your love. Amen.*

Day 21: Preparing for Holy Week

As we approach Holy Week, let us take time to reflect on the significance of these sacred days.

- **Reflecting on the Passion of Christ:**
    - Read the Gospel accounts of Holy Week.
    - Consider the meaning of Christ's suffering and death.
    - Prepare your heart for the celebration of Easter.
- **Prayer for Spiritual Preparation:**
    - *Lord, prepare my heart for Holy Week. Help me to enter more deeply into the mysteries of your passion, death, and resurrection. Amen.*

Holy Week

Palm Sunday: Joy, Humility, and the Cost of Discipleship

Today, we join the crowds as they welcome Jesus into Jerusalem with shouts of praise and waving palm branches. This triumphant entry is a moment of great joy and anticipation. Yet, beneath the surface of this joyful celebration lies a deeper truth: the cost of discipleship.

Jesus, riding on a humble donkey, enters the city not as a conquering king, but as a servant. He comes to fulfill God's will, even though it will lead to suffering and death.

As we celebrate with the crowds today, let us also reflect on the cost of following Christ. Discipleship requires humility, self-denial, and a willingness to embrace the cross.

- **Prayer for Humility and Obedience:**
    - *Lord Jesus, help me to follow you with humility and obedience. Grant me the grace*

to embrace the cross and to live a life that reflects your love. Amen.

Holy Monday & Tuesday: Betrayal and the Sacrament of Love

Holy Monday and Tuesday are days of both anticipation and foreboding. We witness the betrayal of Judas and the preparations for the Passover meal, where Jesus will institute the Eucharist.

- **Faithfulness in the Face of Betrayal:**

    - Reflect on the betrayal of Judas and the importance of faithfulness to God and to one another.
    - Consider how you can remain faithful to Christ in the face of temptation and adversity.
- **The Meaning of the Eucharist:**

    - Recall the Last Supper, where Jesus shared bread and wine with his disciples, instituting the Eucharist, a sacrament of love and remembrance.
    - Prepare to receive Holy Communion with reverence and gratitude.
- **Prayer for Faithfulness and Remembrance:**

- *Lord, help me to remain faithful to you in all circumstances. Help me to receive Holy Communion with reverence and gratitude, remembering your sacrifice and the promise of eternal life. Amen.*

Holy Wednesday: Silence and Reflection

Holy Wednesday is a day of quiet reflection and preparation. As we approach the most solemn days of Holy Week, let us spend time in prayer and contemplation.

- **Seeking God's Presence:**

    - Spend time in quiet prayer, reflecting on the events of the coming days.
    - Read the Gospel accounts of Holy Week and allow the words to sink deeply into your heart.
    - Use this time for introspection and to prepare your heart for the sacred mysteries that lie ahead.

- **Prayer for Reflection and Discernment:**

    - *Lord, grant me the grace to spend this Holy Wednesday in quiet reflection. Help me to prepare my heart for the sacred mysteries of your passion and death. Amen.*

Maundy Thursday: Service and Communion

Maundy Thursday commemorates the Last Supper, where Jesus washed the feet of his disciples, demonstrating the importance of service and humility. He also instituted the Eucharist, a sacrament of love and unity.

- **The Importance of Service:**
    - Reflect on the importance of serving others as an expression of Christian love.
    - Consider how you can serve those in need within your community.
- **The Sacrament of the Eucharist:**
    - Prepare to receive Holy Communion with reverence and gratitude.
    - Remember that the Eucharist is a source of spiritual nourishment and a communion with Christ.
- **Prayer for Service and Communion:**
    - *Lord, help me to serve others with humility and love. Help me to receive Holy Communion with reverence and gratitude, and to experience your presence within me. Amen.*

Good Friday: Contemplating the Cross

Good Friday is a day of sorrow and reflection, a day to contemplate the profound sacrifice of Jesus Christ on the cross.

- **The Significance of the Cross:**
    - Reflect on the meaning of the cross and the depth of God's love for humanity.
    - Consider how Christ's sacrifice has transformed your own life.
- **Prayer for Repentance and Healing:**
    - *Lord, I acknowledge my sins and shortcomings. I thank you for your sacrifice on the cross. Heal the wounds of the world and grant us the grace of your forgiveness. Amen.*

Holy Saturday: Hope in Darkness

Holy Saturday is a day of waiting and anticipation. It is a time to reflect on the silence of the tomb and to trust in God's promise of resurrection.

- **Trusting in God's Promise:**
    - Reflect on the hope of the resurrection and the promise of eternal life.
    - Spend time in prayer, trusting in God's plan and waiting for the dawn of Easter Sunday.
- **Prayer for Hope and Resurrection:**
    - *Lord, in the silence of this day, I place my hope in your promise of resurrection. Grant me the grace to wait patiently and to trust in your divine plan. Amen.*

Easter Sunday

Easter Sunday: Celebrating the Resurrection

Easter Sunday is a day of joy and celebration, a day to rejoice in the resurrection of Jesus Christ.

- **The Meaning of Easter:**
    - Celebrate the victory of Christ over death and the new life that it brings.
    - Reflect on the transforming power of the resurrection and how it affects your own life.
- **Prayer of Thanksgiving and Praise:**
    - *Lord, we praise you for your glorious resurrection! Thank you for the new life you have given us. Fill us with your joy and help us to live lives worthy of the resurrection. Amen.*

Easter Monday: Living the Resurrected Life

Easter Monday is a day to reflect on how we can live out the joy and hope of the resurrection in our daily lives.

- **Living a Resurrected Life:**
    - Let the joy of Easter shine forth in your words and actions.
    - Share the good news of the resurrection with others.
    - Live a life of love, service, and compassion.
- **Prayer for a Transformed Life:**
    - *Lord, help me to live a life transformed by your resurrection. Help me to share the joy of Easter with the world and to be a witness to your love. Amen*

Made in the USA
Columbia, SC
25 March 2025